Great Wisdom and Strategy Collection from ancient China

Dirty Tricks

Jiayan Ying

In loving memory of my father

Dirty tricks are what people use to break the rules in their favour. So why talking about dirty tricks in a book of wisdom?

Naturally, great wisdom should never be cunning; it involves intelligence, deep insight, good sense and so on. However, great wisdom is often brought down by small tricks. To guard against this, a clear understanding of tricks is necessary. And, in any case, a well-used trick can be as effective as great wisdom; tricks can help kingdoms to win battles and protect citizens from their enemies. No one should feel ashamed or afraid to discuss them. Think of our great mountain, Mt Taishan. It may be the highest in the whole country, but that doesn't mean it despises every little pile of sand that dreams of growing into a hill; nor will the ocean mind one little bit if a stream wishes to become a river. And so, even though tricks may seem trivial compared to wisdom, we should never underestimate their power.

Even heroes have been known to lie from time to time. And, don't forget, as the saying goes, there's honour among thieves. Just as wisdom becomes more profound through practice, so does cunning. Evil-doers use cunning to cheat their way to food or drinks; the same cunning, on a larger scale, can bring down a whole kingdom. Therefore, tricks are actually powerful; if you think you don't have the wisdom to fight them at the moment, you'd better learn how to avoid them!

Table of Contents

1   How to steal an empire

吕不韦

秦太子妃曰华阳夫人，无子。夏姬生子异人，质于赵。秦数伐赵，赵不礼之，困不得意。阳翟大贾吕不韦适邯郸，见之曰："此奇货可居。"乃说之曰："太子爱华阳夫人而无子，子之兄弟二十馀人，子居中，不甚见幸，不得争立。不韦请以千金为子西游，立子为嗣。"异人曰："必如君策，秦国与子共之。"不韦乃厚赀西见夫人姊，而以献于夫人，因誉异人贤孝，日夜泣思太子及夫人。不韦因使其姊说曰："夫人爱而无子，异人贤，自知中子不得为适，诚以此时拔之，是异人无国而有国，夫人无子而有子也，则终身有宠于秦矣。"夫人以为然，遂与太子约以为嗣，使不韦还报异人。异人变服逃归，更名楚。不韦娶邯郸姬绝美者与居，知其有娠，异人见而请之，不韦佯怒，既而献之，期年而生子政。嗣楚立，是为始皇。

Long ago – during the period known as The Six Kingdoms – there was a crown prince of the Qin Kingdom who had many wives. His first wife had no son, but several other wives gave birth to boys. One of these boys, called Yi Ren, had been kept as a hostage by the Zhao Kingdom since birth and was having a hard time there. A business man named Lu Buwei, who used to travel between kingdoms for business, heard about his situation and thought to himself: "Yi Ren is a treasure I can make great deal out of."

So, he arranged to meet Yi Ren and told him: you have more than twenty brothers; after all this time that you've been away, your father, the crown prince, is bound to have forgotten all about you. By the time he becomes king, you will have lost any chance to become his heir. But I have a plan. I can help you return home and meet his first wife. Get into her good books and she's sure to beg the prince to make you his heir. Yi Ren agreed and offered to share half of the kingdom with Lu Buwei once he became king.

And so, Yi Ren went home and first met the first wife's sister and won her over by offering her a lot of rare treasures. He also made sure to have plenty of high class people at his house all the time. In this way, Yi Ren soon made a name for himself and people in the kingdom began to think he was something special. When the time was right, Lu Buwei met the crown prince's first wife and told her: you are the favourite wife at the moment which means you have the power to enjoy the life; but without a son, this power cannot last. This young man, Yi Ren, is wise enough to run the kingdom but has less chance than his other brothers. If you two work together, you can make both of your wishes come true and enjoy life forever.

The first wife agreed and made Yi Ren the heir. Lu Buwei made a lot money from this deal and had several pretty women living with him. When one of them became pregnant, he invited Yi Ren over to meet her. Naturally, Yi Ren fell for her and was desperate to bring her back home with him. Lu Buwei put on a great show of anger, but finally gave way and allowed her to marry Yi Ren. When she gave birth to a son, Yi Ren made him his heir. This boy would go on to become the great Emperor Qin who conquered the other five kingdoms, and brought the whole of China under one rule.

And so, you see, the Qin kingdom was the most powerful among all six kingdoms in China at the time. The other kingdoms tried their best to conquer it, going so far as to send an army of a million troops, but still failed. And yet, this one businessman, Lu Buwei, easily conquered the kingdom, without a single battle. In fact, you might call him a thief rather than a businessman!

2　How to get away with a failed conspiracy

徐温

初，张颢与徐温谋弑其节度使杨渥。温曰："参用左右牙兵，必不一，不若独用吾兵。"［边批：反言之。］颢不可。温曰："然则独用公兵。"［边批：本意如此。］颢从之，后穷治逆党，皆左牙兵，由是人以温为实不知谋。

Zhang Jing and Xu Wen were two leaders who had planned to rebel and kill their king. But Xu Wen was having second thoughts. He told Zhang, "If we both lead our soldiers against the king, it may cause confusion because they won't know whose orders to obey. I have a better idea; how about we only use my soldiers for this attack?" This was a clever ploy, because, of course, it made Zhang suspicious; he thought that Xu Wen wanted to take all the glory when the battle was won. So, he replied, "We can just use my soldiers – I'm fine with that." This was actually what Xu wanted all along.

And so, Zhang Jing led his soldiers into battle, but they were defeated. Only Zhang's soldiers were captured and no one even knew that Xu was involved. He got away scot free!

3   How to confirm bad rumours

潘崇

楚成王以商臣为太子，既而又欲立公子职。商臣闻之，未察也。告其傅潘崇曰："若之何而察之。" 潘崇曰："飨江芊成王嬖，而勿敬也。" 商臣从其策，江芊果怒，曰："呼，役夫，宜君王之欲废汝而立职也。" 商臣曰："信矣。"

Once upon a time, the King of the Chu kingdom chose his son Shang as the crown prince. But soon afterwards, Shang heard that his father, the king, had changed his mind, and chosen his brother Zhi instead. However, Shang only heard rumours about this. There had been no official announcement and Shang realised his father might take a long while before making the news public, so he decided he needed to find out for himself. But how? Shang was beside himself with worry, so he went to his great master teacher to seek advice. He explained his predicament and asked, "How can I find out if this rumour is true or not? I can't ask my father and I don't think anyone will tell me even if I do ask."

His great master teacher thought for a while and came up with the following idea. He said, "You should invite your father's favourite wife over for dinner; but do not be nice to her." Shang did as his teacher suggested. The king's wife not supposed to leave the court, but he tempted her with her favourite seafood dishes, so she sneaked out to his place for dinner. During dinner, he was so rude to her that finally she couldn't stand it anymore and burst out, "No wonder your father is going to make Zhi the crown prince instead of you!"

And that's how Shang found out that the rumour was true.

4　How to gain control of the state

田婴　刘谨

田婴相齐，人有说王者曰："终岁之计，王盍以数日之间自听之？不然，无以知吏之奸邪得失也。"王曰："善。"田婴即遽请于王而听其计。王将听之矣，田婴令官具押券斗石参升之计。王自听计，计不胜听。罢食后复坐，不复暮食矣。田婴复请曰："群臣所终岁日夜不敢偷怠之事也，王以一夕听之，则群臣有为劝勉矣。"王曰："诺。"俄而王已睡矣，吏尽偷刀削其押券升石之计。王终不能听，于是尽以委婴。

Here are two stories from different times, which used similar tricks. In the early days of the warrior kingdoms, an official called Tian Ying worked for the Qi kingdom. One day the king was asked if he could spend a few days listening to the last few years' taxation reports, so he would have an idea about the kingdom's economy. The king thought that he'd better accept as it was obviously important state business.

Tian, the official, heard about this and he suggested that the king listen to the kingdom's revenue reports too. Once more, the king agreed. So Tian gathered together all kinds of revenue documents, going into the minutest detail. He then arranged for a treasury official to read these out to the king all day long. By evening the king was exhausted. But Tian said to him, "How inspired our people will be when they hear that their king has been spending so many hours looking after the affairs of the kingdom. They'll surely adore you all the more!" On hearing this flattery, the king kept on listening without a break.

By night time, the king could not keep his eyes open any longer, even though the report was still not finished. He had simply had enough. After such an ordeal, the king asked Tian to take over all responsibility for government revenue, which, of course, was Tian's plan all along.

The same kind of trick was used by another official, called Liu Jin, who served the emperor during the Ming dynasty. Like Tian, he was ambitious for power, so he too came up with a cunning plan. He selected some talented acrobats to put on a show and entertain the emperor. While the Emperor was enjoying the show, Liu arranged for some officials to start reading out important reports for the emperor. This was the last thing the emperor wanted to hear just then, but the officials kept on coming, so eventually he asked Jin if he could deal with them.

After this had happened a few times, the officials got used to reporting important information directly to Jin, rather than the emperor, who had begun to spend less and less time on state business.

5　How to get your money back

严嵩

伊庶人为王时，以残暴历见纠于台使者，迫则行十万余金于嵩，得小缓。及嵩败家居，则遣军卒十辈造嵩家，胁偿金。嵩置酒款之，而好语曰："所惠金十万，实无之，仅得半耳，而又半费，请以二万金偿。"因尽以上所赐金有印识者予之，既去而闻于郡曰："有江盗劫吾家二万金去矣，速掩之，可获也。"郡发卒追得金，悉捕军卒下狱论死。

During the Ming dynasty, there was a brutal and ferocious local ruler named Lord Ying. His misdeeds led to a series of complaints to the Emperor and Lord Ying finally realised that if he didn't find a way to put a stop to these complaints, he would end up in jail. So, he sent a huge bribe of one hundred thousand pieces of gold to the chief justice of the empire, Yan Kao. The bribe did its job and all the charges against Lord Ying were dropped and the complaints were hushed up.

Not long afterwards, the chief justice, Yan Kao, was sacked for some misdeeds of his own and Lord Ying sent ten of his strongmen to Yan's house to demand repayment of the bribe. However, instead of escaping or resisting, Yan Kao put on a great welcome for his visitors, treating them to a feast accompanied by the very best wines. After dinner, he put on a sad face and said, "The truth is, I only received half of the promised bribe. And I have already spent half of what I did receive paying off other court officials when I was charged myself. Please understand my situation. I'm ready to pay back every single piece of gold that I have, which is my last 20, 000. He then gave them the 20, 000 pieces of gold, each one of which had the imperial stamp on it.

As soon as Lord Ying's strongmen had left, Yan Kao went to the government offices to report a robbery. Because the gold he had given the strongmen had the imperial stamp on it, it was very easy to trace. Before long, all the strongmen had been either killed or detained and Yan Gao got his 20, 000 pieces of gold back.

6   How to get rid of rivals

赵高

赵高既劝二世深居，而己专决。李斯病之。高乃见斯曰："关东群盗多，而上益发繇治阿房宫，臣欲谏，为位卑，此真君侯之事，君何不谏？"斯曰："上居深宫，欲见无间。"高曰："请候上间语君。"于是待二世方燕乐，妇女居前，使人告斯："可奏事矣。"斯至上谒，二世怒。高因言丞相怨望欲反，下斯狱，夷三族。

During the last years of the Qin dynasty, the emperor put his servant Zhao Gao in charge of state business. Zhao Gao heard that the prime minister, Li Si, was not happy about his new role. So, one day, when the prime minister was visiting the palace, Zhao Gao said to him: "There have been so many robberies up north, but all the emperor can think about is the new palace he's building for his favourite wife. I really want to speak to him about the robberies, but, you know, I am just a servant, and you are the prime minister. Why don't you say something?"

The Prime Minister, Li Si, replied: "That's exactly what I've been trying to do, but the king leaves the palace so rarely nowadays that I hardly get any chance to speak to him. Actually, I have no idea when he'll be available to see me." On hearing this, Zhao Gao offered to try and set up a meeting between the prime minister and the emperor and Li Si agreed.

And so, one day, just as the emperor was enjoying a party in his palace, Zhao told the prime minister that now was a good time to come and see him. When Li Si arrived at the palace, he asked a servant to tell the emperor that he was there to see him. His unexpected and unwanted visit upset and offended the Emperor, who naturally sent him on his way. While the emperor was in this mood, Zhao Gao let him know that Li Si had been complaining about his behaviour and boasting about how he was going to put a stop to it. Well, this sent the Emperor into such a rage that he ordered Li Si to be thrown into jail and his whole family killed.

7   More ways to get rid of rivals

李林甫

李林甫谓李适之曰："华山有金矿，采之可以益国，上未之知也。"［边批：使金果可采，林甫何不自言？］他日适之言之，上以问林甫，对曰："臣久知之，但华山陛下本命，王气所在，凿之非宜，故不敢言。"上以林甫为爱己，而疏适之，遂罢政事。严挺之徙绛州刺史。天宝初，帝顾林甫曰："严挺之安在？此其才可用。"林甫退召其弟损之，与道旧，谆谆款曲，且许美官，因曰："天子视绛州厚要，当以事自解归，得见上，且大用。"边批：天子果欲大用，何待见乎？因绐挺之使称疾，愿就医京师。林甫已得奏，即言挺之春秋高，有疾，幸闲官得养。帝恨咤久之，乃以为员外詹事，诏归东郡。挺之郁郁成疾。帝尝大陈乐勤政楼，既罢，兵部侍郎卢绚按辔绝道去。帝爱其蕴藉，称美之。明日，林甫召绚子，曰："尊府素望，上欲任以交、广，若惮行，且当请老。"绚惧，从之，因出为华州刺史，绚由是废。

Here are two stories about a government official, known as Li Lin Pu, who served the emperor during the Tang dynasty. He became famous for using mind games to get what he wanted.

He had a rival in the government – a rather simple-minded man called Li Shi Zhi, who was in charge of law enforcement. One day, Li Lin Pu told him that there were secret gold mines under the great mountain, Mt Huashan. "Just imagine the wealth it would bring us if only the Emperor allowed those mines to be opened!"

The first thing Li Shi Zhi did, of course, was to go straight to the emperor and tell him all about it. Naturally, the emperor was very interested in Li Shi Zhi's news, but before starting out on such a huge enterprise, he decided to seek Li Lin Pu's advice. Li Lin Pu told him, "Oh, those mines? I've known about them for a long while, but opening them up again? I'd never dream of doing such a thing. We all know that the great mountain represents you. Therefore, doing harm to the mountain is like harming the great emperor himself. And that's something I would never suggest." This display of loyalty mightily impressed the emperor and made him think twice about Li Shi Zhu. After that, he began to cut him off and transfer responsibility for state business to Li Lin Pu.

On another occasion, the emperor decided to re-employ a highly talented court official named Yan Ting Zhu who had worked for him long before, but had been demoted to commoner status because of some mistakes he had made. The emperor he asked Li Lin Pu to find him and bring him back to the palace. Li Lin Pu didn't like this idea at all. Anyway, as he knew that Yan Ting Zhu's younger brother was still working for the government, he went to meet him and spoke kindly about his family, including his brother, Yan Ting Zhi.

He told him, "The king is very concerned about your brother. Let's arrange for him to come back here. The more the king sees of him, the more he'll remember the good old days and the wonderful service your brother had provided. The king will surely give him a second chance. All we need is a good excuse for him to return to town. How about if he writes a letter to the king, saying that he's very sick and needs to come back for urgent medical attention?"

He did so, and Li Lin Pu showed the letter to the king, explaining that it was clear that Yan was not only getting on in years, but clearly frail. "If he comes back to work for you, how can he deal with the stress of major state business? How about offering him some small tasks instead, out of the goodness of your heart?"

The king sighed and reluctantly agreed. And so, when Yan did return, he was left waiting in vain for the king to come and meet him. As a result, he became ill for real.

8   How to get away with cuckolding the Emperor

达奚盈盈

达奚盈盈者，天宝中贵人之妾，姿艳冠绝一时。会同官之子为千牛者失，索之甚急。明皇闻之，诏大索京师，无所不至，而莫见其迹。因问近往何处，其父言："贵人病，尝往候之。"诏且索贵人之室，盈盈谓千牛曰："今势不能自隐矣，出亦无甚害。"千牛惧得罪，盈盈因教曰："第不可言在此，如上问何往，但云所见人物如此，所见帘幕帷帐如此，所食物如此，势不由己，决无患矣。"既出，明皇大怒，问之，对如盈盈言，上笑而不问。[边批：错认了。]后数日，虢国夫人入内，上戏谓曰："何久藏少年不出耶？"夫人亦大笑而已。[亦错认。]

Back in the days of the Tang dynasty, there was a beautiful and elegant young woman known as Da Xi Ying Ying. She was the most striking beauty in the whole empire and, naturally, became one of the emperor's wives. She had a special friend of her own - a handsome young man called Qian Niu, who was the son of a court official. One day, he heard that Da Xi was sick, so he told his family he would pay her a visit. When he failed to return, his family became very worried and searched high and low, to no avail.

Eventually, the emperor himself became involved. He asked the family where their son, Qian Niu, had gone to and when they told him that he had been to visit Da Xi because she was sick, he ordered his soldiers to search his own palace. They returned empty-handed, as Qian Niu had somehow managed to hide in Da Xi's room. But the fact that the emperor himself was involved made the two young 'friends' very anxious.

This was when Da Xi came up with a cunning plan. What Qian Niu had to do was simply present himself to the Emperor and explain that he'd been detained by a beautiful woman. He should explain that this woman had treated him very well indeed, giving him the very best food and wine. He must describe the woman's room in great detail, including the beautiful decorations, the candles, the colour of the curtains, and even the gorgeous fabric of the bedding.

And so, following Da Xi's highly precise instructions, Qian went to see the emperor the very next day. The emperor was naturally rather angry, not to mention, curious, and demanded an explanation. Qian replied exactly as Da Xi had suggested and, to his surprise, the emperor relaxed and a knowing smile spread across his lips. He had no further questions for the young man.

A few days later, however, the emperor did have a question – not for the young man, but for his sister in law, Lady Jiang Guo, who happened to be visiting the palace. He asked, while giving her a knowing wink, 'What are you doing? Are you hiding all the good looking young men away in your room?' Lady Jiang Guo gasped, but did not utter a word; her only response was a somewhat embarrassed smile. That was enough for the emperor – now he had no doubt where Qian had been hiding all this time.

But how did Da Xi come up with such a plan? Well, she had a good idea that Lady Jiang Guo enjoyed the intimate company, let's say, of a number of gentlemen - including the emperor himself. And the emperor knew full well of her various dalliances. So when he asked her about Qian, she assumed he was teasing her – that was why she said nothing. And, given her reputation and his fondness for her, the emperor naturally decided to 'let her have her fun'. And that was the end of it!

9 How to separate the sheep from the goats

韩昭侯 子之

韩昭侯握瓜而佯亡一瓜，求之甚急。左右因割其瓜而效之，昭侯以此察左右之诚。子之相燕，坐而佯言曰："走出门者何白马也。"左右皆言不见，有一人走追之，报曰："有。"子之以此知左右之不诚信

These two stories show how leaders used small, apparently insignificant events, to find out which of their followers was truly loyal to them: in other words, to separate the sheep from the goats.

In one case, a leader named Han Zhao Hou was eating a melon in the company of his allies. On purpose, he dropped the melon on the ground and put on a disappointed expression. In an instant, one of his allies had offered him his own melon to eat. And from this seemingly trivial incident, he found out who he could trust to stand by him in times of need.

Another leader known as Zi Zhi used a similar tactic. He was the right-hand man of the warrior king Yan. One day, Zi Zhu was sitting in the hall with his soldiers. All of a sudden he asked, "Did any one see a white horse go through the door just now?" The soldiers in the hall just looked around and said they hadn't seen a thing. Just one of them leapt to his feet and ran outside to check. A few minutes later, he came back, out of breath, saying that indeed, he had managed to see the white horse. Once again, a simple test showed who was really willing to serve.

10 How to hedge your bets

綦毋恢

韩咎立为君，未定也，弟在周，周欲重之，而恐韩之不立也。

[不立其弟。] 綦毋恢曰：“不若以车百乘送之。得立，因曰为戒；不立，则曰来效贼也。”

During the age of the warring states, the King of the Han Kingdom passed away. His likely heir was his eldest son, Zhe; however, this had not been officially confirmed. As it happened, there was another son who might well have a claim on the throne. He was living away from home, in the Zhou Kingdom and, naturally, the government there wanted to support his claim, for their own interests.

The problem for the Zhou government was that they had no clear idea of what decision had been made about the new King of the Han. Ideally, the Zhou wanted their preferred candidate on the throne, but not at the risk of provoking their powerful neighbour if they had misjudged the situation. They needed a plan that would somehow succeed whatever the Han Kingdom decided.

Finally, a clever court official solved their dilemma. All they needed to do was to send the younger brother back to the Han Kingdom with an armed guard of hundreds of soldiers. If it turned out that this younger brother had been chosen as the new king, they could say they had protected him every inch of the perilous journey home. If, on the other hand, the elder brother had been chosen, they could say that they had escorted this dangerous traitor back home to face justice.

11 How to avoid trouble by doing nothing

苏代

苏代自燕之齐，见于章华南门。齐王曰："嘻，子之来也！秦使魏冉致帝，子以为何如？"对曰："王之问臣也卒，而患之所从生者微。今不听，是恨秦也；听之，是恨天下也。不如听之以为秦，勿庸称之以为天下。秦称之，天下听之，主亦称之；先后之事，帝名为无伤也。秦称之而天下不听，王因勿称，于以收天下，此大资也。"

As we have seen, the period of the warring states was a very delicate time in which governments were faced with all kinds of tricky dilemmas requiring ingenious solutions. One such case involved the Qi Kingdom that was coming under increasing pressure from the powerful Qin Kingdom. Fortunately, just at this time, one of their wisest men, Su Dai, returned home from his travels.

The King immediately went to see him and demanded to know why he had taken so long to return when his country needed him. Anyway, he now needed his urgent advice, since he had just received a messenger from the Qin Kingdom requesting that they announce publicly that they accepted the Qin King's claim to be acknowledged as an emperor of the whole of China. What should he do?

Su's answer: Nothing at all! "You see," he explained, "the question is too sudden and the whole issue of relationships between kingdoms is just too hot to handle right now. Who knows what will happen next? If you refuse this request, the Qin Kingdom will surely regard you as an enemy; but if you accept, you're just as sure to turn all the other kingdoms against you.

The fact is that, in situations like this, where any action is dangerous, the only sensible thing is to do nothing but wait. If the Qin King starts to call himself emperor, and none of the other kings object, then you can do likewise. But if the other kings all line up in opposition, then you'll know it's safe to ignore the request. Only time will tell.

12 How to find out the king's favourite

薛公

齐王夫人死。有七孺子皆近，薛公欲知王所立，乃献七珥，美其一，明日视美珥所在，劝王立为夫人。

As we've mentioned before, in olden days, the rulers of China had many wives; however, they chose one of these to be their Queen or Empress. And if she died, it could be difficult to choose the next one from among the remaining wives. And so, for this reason, the King of the Qi Kingdom sought the advice of a trusted servant, Xue Gong.

The problem was that Xue Gong really had no idea who the King's favourite wife was. Naturally, he was afraid that if he recommended the wrong one, he could end up in serious trouble; his family too. What he needed was a sure way of finding out which wife was truly the King's favourite, so that he could recommend the one who the King was probably thinking of anyway.

Here's how he went about it. He gave the king seven precious earrings as a gift, among which one was especially beautiful. The next day, when he visited the palace, all he needed to do was to see which of the King's wives was wearing it. There was no risk in recommending her as the next Queen.

13 How to put an end to piracy

唐类函

吴中地方出版商的利润很大，因此从事翻刻（即今日的盗印）的人也特别多，为此出版商相当苦恼。俞羡章所编著的《唐类函》，尚未出版，他便一状告到官府，假称他的新书出版后，用车载往他处时遭盗匪劫走，希望官府派吏卒缉捕盗匪，他并且出钱悬赏缉捕盗书贼。这件事轰动一时，结果使《唐类函》大为畅销，而且也没有书局再敢翻刻。

There was once a flourishing publishing centre in a place called Wu Zhong. However, just as happens today, illegal copying was eating into the profits of both publishers and authors.

But one of these authors found a perfect way to boost sales and, at the same time, stop anyone else from profiting from his work. What he did was to report the theft of his new book even before it had been published.

To help the authorities to bring the thieves to justice, he offered a huge reward to anyone who could catch them. This huge reward put off anyone from copying the book for fear of being caught and punished for armed robbery. At the same time, it was great publicity for his new book!

14 How to make the most of unwanted land

窦公

唐崇贤窦公善治生，而力甚困。京城内有隙地一段，与大阉相邻，阉贵欲之，然其地止值五六百千而已。窦公欣然以此奉之，殊不言价。阉既喜甚，乃托故欲往江淮，希三两护戎缄题。阉为致书，凡获三千缗，由是甚济。东市有隙地一片，洼下停污，乃以廉值市之，俾婢妪将蒸饼盘就彼诱儿童，若抛砖瓦中一指标，得一饼。儿童奔走竞抛，十填六七，乃以好土覆之，起一店停波斯，日获一缗。

During the Tang dynasty, there was a smart business man called Dou Gong who had a particularly creative approach to property speculation.

For instance, one day he was wandering around the country as he usually did, looking for opportunities, when he came across a luxurious mansion set in beautiful grounds. He made some inquiries and found out that it belonged to an official who worked in the capital for the king.

He noticed that right next to this fine estate, there was a dirty, neglected pond, so he found the owner and bought it for next to nothing. He then borrowed some money and set about improving it; he cleaned it up, filled it with fish, fenced it in and planted pretty flowers all around.

Then he simply waited for the government official to visit his estate during his holiday. Naturally, on seeing the now beautiful pond next to his estate, he fell in love with it and sought out Dou Gong to make him an offer. However, Dou Gong refused any payment, insisting that the official must take the pond as a gift. This was the start of a firm friendship between the two men.

 Not long afterwards, Dou Gong told the official that he had decided to travel down south in search of adventure. The official insisted on writing letters of recommendation to all the important people in the south, instructing them to take good care of his friend. And so, Dou Gong did very well down south, making himself a small fortune with all the support he received.

That was not the only time when Dou Gong saw a way of making a fortune from an unwanted piece of land. On another occasion, he came across a site which no one wanted because it was riddled with holes which filled up with water on rainy days. Once again, he bought it for next to nothing and set about improving. This time, what he did was put targets behind each of the holes and invite the local children to try to hit them by throwing stones across the holes. If they did manage the hit the target, they could win a piece of cake. This proved very popular and before long, the kids were lining up to throw stones. Of course, most of them fell short of the targets and began filling up the holes.

After a few months, there were no holes left and Dou Gong was able to build 20 shops on the land. These attracted Persian businessmen, doing lucrative international trade, and, naturally, producing substantial profits for Dou Gong.

15 How to obtain a free travel upgrade

黠童子

一童子随主人宦游。从县中索骑，彼所值甚驽下。望后来人得骏马，驰而来，手握缰绳，佯泣于马上。后来问曰："何泣也？"曰："吾马奔逸绝尘，深惧其泛驾而伤我也。"后来以为稚弱可信，意此马更佳，乃下地与之易。童子既得马，策而去，后来人乘马，始悟其欺，追之不及。

There was a young servant who needed to ride to a faraway town to help his boss to find a job there. However, the horse he'd been given to ride was slow and uncomfortable, so he became determined to try to get a better one. So, when he saw another rider approaching, he jumped off the horse and started walking alongside, holding the reins as tightly as he could and crying his eyes out. The other man stopped and asked what was going on. The boy explained that his horse was so strong and fast that he was too scared to ride it because he was bound to lose control and be thrown off. He was at his wit's end.

The man thought he could take advantage of this helpless, innocent boy, who was obviously too young to make up lies. So, he offered to help the boy out by exchanging horses with him. As soon as the man handed over his horse, the boy jumped into the saddle and rode away. Of course, as soon as the man got on the decrepit horse which the boy had given him, he realised he had been deceived. But by this time, the boy and his horse were disappearing into the distance.

16 How to deal with a wicked stepmother

术制继母

王阳明年十二，继母待之不慈。父官京师。公度不能免，以母信佛，乃夜潜起，列五托子于室门。母晨兴，见而心悸。他日复如之，母愈骇，然犹不悛也。公乃于郊外访射鸟者，得一异形鸟，生置母衾母。母整衾，见怪鸟飞去，大惧，召巫媪问之。公怀金赂媪，诈言"王状元前室责母虐其遗婴，今诉于天，遣阴兵收妆魂魄。衾中之鸟是也。"后母大恸，叩头谢不敢，公亦泣拜良久。巫故作恨恨，乃蹶然苏。自是母性骤变。

A collection of traditional tales would not be complete without at least one account of a wicked stepmother. This one featured a young boy, just twelve years old, called Wang Yang Ming. His cruel stepmother often mistreated him, and he couldn't complain to his father because his work took him far away from home and he rarely even returned. And so, Wang realised he was going to have to help himself.

Knowing that his stepmother was a Buddhist, he used this as a way of putting her in her place. One night, he got up quietly, without waking anyone and went to the living room. He took the tea tray that was there and put it outside the room where his stepmother used to pray. The next morning, when she saw it there, she got a fright. But this alone didn't stop her mistreating the boy.

So Wang decided to go one step further. He went to the
countryside and bought an unusual tame but ugly looking bird.
When he got back home, he put this bird under his stepmother's
bedsheet. When she went to make her bed, the bird flew out and
gave her a huge scare.

She decided that she need to find out what was going on, so,
being superstitious, she went out and found a witch who could
visit the home and help her investigate. However, it was actually
Wang himself who had arranged for the witch to be waiting for
his stepmother to find her.

The witch visited the house and told the stepmother that all of
the strange events were being brought about by Wang's real
mother who had died some time before. This poor woman had
seen how the stepmother had been treating her son and
complained to the king in heaven. The bird she'd found was one
of the soldiers he had sent down to arrest her.

This did the trick. The stepmother was scared to death and knelt
down begging Wang for forgiveness. Being a kind – and clever –
young boy, he said nothing, but knelt down himself and begged
her for forgiveness too. The witch sighed and left. From that day
on, Wang's stepmother treated him as if he were her own son.

17 How to accept a bribe without risk or return

下马常例

宋时有世赏官王氏，任浙西一监。初莅任日，吏民献钱物几数百千，仍白曰"下马常例"。王公见之，以为污己，便欲作状，并物申解上司。吏辈祈请再四。乃令取一柜，以物悉纳其中，对众封缄，置于厅治，戒曰："有一小犯，即发！"由是吏民惊惧，课息俱备。比终任荣归，登舟之次，吏白厅柜。公曰："寻常既有此例，须有文牍。"吏赍案至，俾舁柜于舟，载之而去。

During the Song dynasty, there was a government official named Wang who had been put in charge of a district in the far west of the empire. The local staff were determined to make a positive impression on their new boss, so they prepared a lavish gift for him, made up of hundreds of thousands of gold coins.

On seeing all this gold, Wang was disturbed. If he accepted this gift, it would undermine his authority. They would expect him to do whatever they wanted, or at least to be easy on them. So, he put on a furious expression and threatened to report them all to the imperial government.

The local official hurriedly explained that the gift was just a traditional way of welcoming a guest; nothing more than that. So Wang accepted the gift, but demanded that the coins be boxed up and stored in a storeroom, where no one could touch them. At the same time, he made it clear that if any of the local officials stepped out of line, they would be reported to the central government.

This had the required effect. The local officials were so frightened that they did everything by the book, under his strict supervision. Eventually, the time came for him to leave and return to the capital. Before going, some of the local officials reminded him of the gold. He had prepared for this moment. He told them that as it was a traditional custom of the region, he had no reason to refuse their gift, but that they needed to provide him with written confirmation of this. And so, with this in hand, he returned home laden with gold, but with a clean conscience.

18 How to pull off a dirty deal

谢生

长洲谢生嗜酒，尝游张幼于先生之门。幼于喜宴会，而家贫不能醉客。一日得美酒招客，童子率斟半杯，谢生苦不足，因出席小遗，纸封土块，招童子密授之，嘱曰："我因脏病发，不能饮，今以数文钱劳汝，求汝浅斟吾酒也。"发封得块，恨甚，故满斟之，谢是日独得倍饮。

There was a man called Xie Sheng who loved a drink. He especially used to enjoy drinking at his friend Zhang's house, because he was pleasant company. However, there was one serious drawback; Zhang was stingy with his drink. That is to say, he himself had a full glass, but had instructed his boy servant to provide his guests with half a glass.

Eventually, Xie decided he had enough of this and was going to do something about it. So the next time he was invited to Zhang's house, along with some other guests, he didn't drink the half glass which the boy poured for him. Instead, he excused himself to go to the bathroom. However, what he actually did was to go outside and pick up some dirt from the ground. He wrapped this up in paper and returned to the party.

When the boy servant came out again, he handed him the package, telling him, "I've a pain in my kidney today, so I'm afraid I can't drink much. But here is some money for you. Why don't you go and buy yourself some nice teas?" And he made a point of reminding the boy not, on any account, to pour too much wine for him.

As soon as Xie Sheng left the house, the boy tore open the package and found, to his dismay, that it was full of dirt. He cursed Xie, but got the message. After that, he made sure to pour Xie a full glass every time and, naturally, Xie ended up drinking a lot more than any of the other guests.

I gathered together a number of little stories about miscellaneous tricks, so that, together, they might add up to some great wisdom
for daily life.

End.